CH00820960

To:

From:

Message:

Published by Christian Art Publishers
PO Box 1599, Vereeniging, 1930, RSA

© 2019
First edition 2019

Designed by Christian Art Publishers

Images used under license from Shutterstock.com

Printed in China

ISBN 978-1-4321-3083-1

19 20 21 22 23 24 25 26 27 28 – 10 9 8 7 6 5 4 3 2 1

THE
Serenity
Prayer
PROMISE BOOK

CHRISTIAN ART PUBLISHERS

God grant me

the *serenity* to *accept*

the things I cannot change;

courage to change the things I can;

and *wisdom* to know the difference.

Living *one day* at a time;

enjoying *one moment* at a time;

accepting hardships as the

pathway to *peace;*

taking, as He did,

this sinful world as it is,

not as I would have it;

trusting that He will make

all things *right*

if I surrender to His will;

that I may be reasonably *happy*

in this *life* and supremely happy

with *Him* forever in the next.

Amen.

Contents

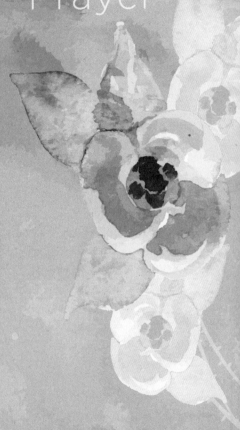

Serenity
Prayer

God grant me the

serenity

to accept

the things I cannot change.

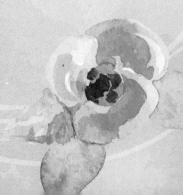

1.
Praying for Serenity

The prayer of a righteous person
is powerful and effective.

James 5:16 NIV

Devote yourselves to prayer with
an alert mind and a thankful heart.

Colossians 4:2 NLT

Pray in the Spirit on all occasions
with all kinds of prayers and requests.
With this in mind, be alert and always
keep on praying for all
the Lord's people.

Ephesians 6:18 NIV

"When you pray, go into your room,
close the door and pray to your
Father, who is unseen. Then your
Father, who sees what is done in
secret, will reward you."

Matthew 6:6 NIV

The LORD delights in the
prayers of the upright.

Proverbs 15:8 NLT

"When you pray, do not use vain
repetitions as the heathen do.
For they think that they will be
heard for their many words.
Therefore do not be like them.
For your Father knows the things
you have need of before you
ask Him."

Matthew 6:7-8 NKJV

Is anyone among you in trouble?
Let them pray. Is anyone happy?
Let them sing songs of praise.
Is anyone among you sick?
Let them call the elders of the
church to pray over them and
anoint them with oil in
the name of the Lord.

James 5:13-14 NIV

"If you believe, you will receive
whatever you ask for in prayer."

Matthew 21:22 NIV

This is the confidence that
we have in Him, that if we ask
anything according to His will,
He hears us. And if we know that
He hears us, whatever we ask,
we know that we have the petitions
that we have asked of Him.

1 John 5:14-15 NKJV

The eyes of the Lord are on the
righteous and His ears are
attentive to their prayer.

1 Peter 3:12 NIV

"I tell you, you can pray for
anything, and if you believe that
you've received it, it will be yours."

Mark 11:24 NLT

Truly God has listened; He has
attended to the voice of my prayer.
Blessed be God, because He has
not rejected my prayer or removed
His steadfast love from me!

Psalm 66:19-20 ESV

Do what you can and pray for what you cannot yet do.

ST. AUGUSTINE

2.

Blessed Assurance

Blessed are those whose way
is blameless, who walk in
the law of the Lord!

Psalm 119:1 ESV

"God blesses those who are poor
and realize their need for Him,
for the Kingdom of Heaven is theirs."

Matthew 5:3 NLT

"Bring all the tithes into the
storehouse so there will be enough
food in My Temple. If you do,"
says the Lord of Heaven's Armies,
"I will open the windows of heaven
for you. I will pour out a blessing
so great you won't have enough
room to take it in! Try it!
Put Me to the test!"

Malachi 3:10 NLT

Taste and see that the Lord is good;
blessed is the one who takes
refuge in Him.

Psalm 34:8 NIV

The Lord will indeed give what is good,
and our land will yield its harvest.

Psalm 85:12 NIV

"Blessed are the pure in heart,
for they shall see God."

Matthew 5:8 NKJV

When You open Your hand,
You satisfy the hunger and thirst of
every living thing. The Lord is
righteous in everything He does;
He is filled with kindness.

Psalm 145:16-17 NLT

The blessing of the Lord brings wealth,
without painful toil for it.

Proverbs 10:22 NIV

"Blessed are the meek,
for they will inherit the earth."

Matthew 5:5 NIV

The LORD bless you and keep you; the LORD make His face shine upon you, and be gracious to you; the LORD lift up His countenance upon you, and give you peace.

Numbers 6:24-26 NKJV

"God blesses those who are merciful, for they will be shown mercy."

Matthew 5:7 NLT

The LORD is my chosen portion and my cup; You hold my lot. The lines have fallen for me in pleasant places; indeed, I have a beautiful inheritance.

Psalm 16:5-6 ESV

All praise to God, the Father of our Lord Jesus Christ, who has blessed us with every spiritual blessing in the heavenly realms because we are united with Christ.

Ephesians 1:3 NLT

When we lose one blessing, another is often most unexpectedly given in its place.

C. S. LEWIS

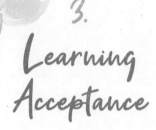

3.
Learning Acceptance

Accept one another, then,
just as Christ accepted you,
in order to bring praise to God.

Romans 15:7 NIV

Accept other believers who are
weak in faith, and don't argue
with them about what they think
is right or wrong.

Romans 14:1 NLT

"Anyone who welcomes you welcomes
Me, and anyone who welcomes Me
welcomes the one who sent Me."

Matthew 10:40 NIV

"All those the Father gives Me will
come to Me, and whoever comes
to Me I will never drive away."

John 6:37 NIV

So why do you condemn another believer? Why do you look down on another believer? Remember, we will all stand before the judgment seat of God. For the Scriptures say, "'As surely as I live,' says the LORD, 'every knee will bend to Me, and every tongue will declare allegiance to God.'" Yes, each of us will give a personal account to God.

Romans 14:10-12 NLT

Put on then, as God's chosen ones, holy and beloved, compassionate hearts, kindness, humility, meekness, and patience, bearing with one another and, if one has a complaint against another, forgiving each other.

Colossians 3:12-13 ESV

It is a good thing to receive wealth from God and the good health to enjoy it. To enjoy your work and accept your lot in life – this is indeed a gift from God.

Ecclesiastes 5:19 NLT

Since everything God created
is good, we should not reject any
of it but receive it with thanks.

1 Timothy 4:4 NLT

You will be accepted
if you do what is right.

Genesis 4:7 NLT

Finally, all of you, be like-minded,
be sympathetic, love one another,
be compassionate and humble.
Do not repay evil with evil or insult
with insult. On the contrary, repay
evil with blessing, because to this
you were called so that you may
inherit a blessing.

1 Peter 3:8-9 NIV

Let us consider one another in order
to stir up love and good works,
not forsaking the assembling of
ourselves together, as is the manner
of some, but exhorting one another,
and so much the more as you see
the Day approaching.

Hebrews 10:24-25 NKJV

To keep the
Golden Rule
we must put
ourselves in other
people's places,
but to do that
consists in and
depends upon
picturing ourselves
in their places.

HARRY EMERSON FOSDICK

4.
Faith in God's Plan

"I tell you the truth, if you had faith
even as small as a mustard seed,
you could say to this mountain,
'Move from here to there,'
and it would move.
Nothing would be impossible."

Matthew 17:20 NLT

Now faith is the substance of things
hoped for, the evidence
of things not seen.

Hebrews 11:1 NKJV

Because of Christ and our faith in Him,
we can now come boldly and
confidently into God's presence.

Ephesians 3:12 NLT

Be on your guard; stand firm in
the faith; be courageous; be strong.

1 Corinthians 16:13 NIV

We fix our eyes not on what is seen,
but on what is unseen, since what
is seen is temporary, but what
is unseen is eternal.

2 Corinthians 4:18 NIV

In all circumstances take up the
shield of faith, with which you can
extinguish all the flaming darts
of the evil one.

Ephesians 6:16 ESV

For in the gospel the righteousness
of God is revealed – a righteousness
that is by faith from first to last,
just as it is written:
"The righteous will live by faith."

Romans 1:17 NIV

I have fought the good fight,
I have finished the race,
I have kept the faith.

2 Timothy 4:7 NIV

Faith comes from hearing the
message, and the message is heard
through the word about Christ.

Romans 10:17 NIV

"Anyone who believes and
is baptized will be saved.
But anyone who refuses
to believe will be condemned."

Mark 16:16 NLT

But as for you, continue in what you
have learned and have firmly
believed, knowing from whom
you learned it.

2 Timothy 3:14 ESV

Without faith it is impossible to
please Him, for he who comes to
God must believe that He is,
and that He is a rewarder of
those who diligently seek Him.

Hebrews 11:6 NKJV

Everyone who believes that
Jesus is the Christ has been born
of God, and everyone who loves
the Father loves whoever
has been born of Him.

1 John 5:1 ESV

God always gives His best to those who leave the choice with Him.

JIM ELLIOT

5.
A Humble Heart

Humble yourselves in the sight
of the Lord, and He will lift you up.

James 4:10 NKJV

True humility and fear of the LORD
lead to riches, honor, and long life.

Proverbs 22:4 NLT

Clothe yourselves, all of you,
with humility toward one another,
for "God opposes the proud
but gives grace to the humble."
Humble yourselves, therefore, under
the mighty hand of God so that
at the proper time He may exalt you.

1 Peter 5:5-6 ESV

"I will bless those who have
humble and contrite hearts,
who tremble at My word."

Isaiah 66:2 NLT

"He who is greatest among you shall be your servant. And whoever exalts himself will be humbled, and he who humbles himself will be exalted."

Matthew 23:11-12 NKJV

"Truly, I say to you, unless you turn and become like children, you will never enter the kingdom of heaven. Whoever humbles himself like this child is the greatest in the kingdom of heaven."

Matthew 18:3-4 ESV

Pride leads to disgrace, but with humility comes wisdom.

Proverbs 11:2 NLT

He has shown you, O mortal, what is good. And what does the LORD require of you? To act justly and to love mercy and to walk humbly with your God.

Micah 6:8 NIV

Pride ends in humiliation,
while humility brings honor.

Proverbs 29:23 NLT

Do nothing out of selfish ambition
or vain conceit. Rather, in humility
value others above yourselves,
not looking to your own interests
but each of you to the interests
of the others.

Philippians 2:3-4 NIV

The Lord supports the humble,
but He brings the wicked
down into the dust.

Psalm 147:6 NLT

Seek the Lord, all you humble
of the land, you who do what He
commands. Seek righteousness,
seek humility.

Zephaniah 2:3 NIV

Haughtiness goes before
destruction; humility
precedes honor.

Proverbs 18:12 NLT

True humility
is able
to look at God
and proceed on.

WATCHMAN NEE

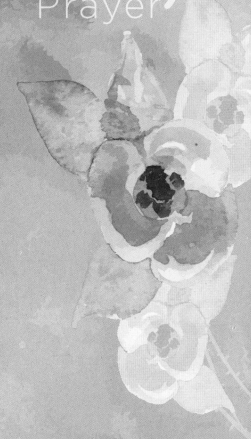

Serenity Prayer

God grant me the

courage

to change the things I can;

and *wisdom*

to know the difference.

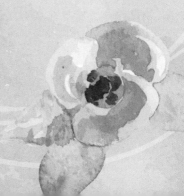

6.

Courage Enough for Today

"Be strong and courageous.
Do not be afraid; do not be
discouraged, for the Lord your God
will be with you wherever you go."

Joshua 1:9 NIV

Be strong and of good courage,
do not fear nor be afraid of them;
for the Lord your God, He is the
One who goes with you. He will not
leave you nor forsake you.

Deuteronomy 31:6 NKJV

In Your strength I can crush an army;
with my God I can scale any wall.

Psalm 18:29 NLT

Be strong in the Lord and
in His mighty power.

Ephesians 6:10 NIV

If God is for us,
who can ever be against us?

Romans 8:31 NLT

Surely the righteous will never
be shaken; they will be remembered
forever. They will have no fear of
bad news; their hearts are steadfast,
trusting in the Lord.

Psalm 112:6-7 NIV

Take courage! For I believe God.
It will be just as He said.

Acts 27:25 NLT

When I am afraid, I put my trust in
You. In God, whose word I praise,
in God I trust; I shall not be afraid.
What can flesh do to me?

Psalm 56:3-4 ESV

Be of good courage, and let us be
strong for our people and for the
cities of our God. And may the
Lord do what is good in His sight.

2 Samuel 10:12 NKJV

Jesus immediately said to them:
"Take courage! It is I.
Don't be afraid."

Matthew 14:27 NIV

Be strong and courageous and do it.
Do not be afraid and do not be
dismayed, for the LORD God,
even my God, is with you. He will
not leave you or forsake you.

1 Chronicles 28:20 ESV

Do not be afraid. Stand firm
and you will see the deliverance
the LORD will bring you today.

Exodus 14:13 NIV

Yea, though I walk through
the valley of the shadow of death,
I will fear no evil; for You are with
me; Your rod and Your staff,
they comfort me.

Psalm 23:4 NKJV

Do not ask for
fears to be
removed;
ask for courage
equal to the fears.

JACK HYLES

7.

Giving It My All

Whatever you do, do it heartily,
as to the Lord and not to men.

Colossians 3:23 NKJV

"Be strong, all you people of the land,"
says the LORD, "and work; for I am
with you," says the LORD of hosts.

Haggai 2:4 NKJV

You shall eat the fruit of the labor of
your hands; you shall be blessed,
and it shall be well with you.

Psalm 128:2 ESV

Whatever you do, in word or deed,
do everything in the name of the
Lord Jesus, giving thanks to
God the Father through Him.

Colossians 3:17 NIV

God is not unjust. He will not forget
how hard you have worked for Him
and how you have shown your love
to Him by caring for other believers,
as you still do.

Hebrews 6:10 NLT

I can do all things through
Christ who strengthens me.

Philippians 4:13 NKJV

My dear brothers and sisters,
be strong and immovable.
Always work enthusiastically for the
Lord, for you know that nothing you
do for the Lord is ever useless.

1 Corinthians 15:58 NLT

Let the favor of the Lord our God
be upon us, and establish the work
of our hands upon us; yes, establish
the work of our hands!

Psalm 90:17 ESV

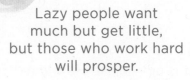

Lazy people want
much but get little,
but those who work hard
will prosper.

Proverbs 13:4 NLT

Work brings profit, but mere talk
leads to poverty! Wealth is a
crown for the wise; the effort of
fools yields only foolishness.

Proverbs 14:23-24 NLT

"Do not labor for the food which
perishes, but for the food which
endures to everlasting life,
which the Son of Man will give you,
because God the Father has set
His seal on Him."

John 6:27 NKJV

Work hard and become a leader;
be lazy and become a slave.

Proverbs 12:24 NLT

There is nothing better than to
enjoy food and drink and to find
satisfaction in work ... these
pleasures are from the hand of God.

Ecclesiastes 2:24 NLT

It is our best work that God wants ... I think He must prefer quality to quantity.

GEORGE MACDONALD

8.
Seeking
Wisdom from Above

If you need wisdom, ask our generous
God, and He will give it to you.
He will not rebuke you for asking.

James 1:5 NLT

The entrance of Your words
gives light; it gives understanding
to the simple.

Psalm 119:130 NKJV

"I will instruct you and teach you in
the way you should go; I will counsel
you with My loving eye on you."

Psalm 32:8 NIV

The wisdom that comes from heaven
is first of all pure; then peace-loving,
considerate, submissive, full of mercy
and good fruit, impartial and sincere.

James 3:17 NIV

Wisdom is sweet to your soul.
If you find it, you will have a bright
future, and your hopes will not
be cut short.

Proverbs 24:14 NLT

For the Lord gives wisdom;
from His mouth come knowledge
and understanding.

Proverbs 2:6 NIV

Listen to counsel and receive
instruction, that you may
be wise in your latter days.

Proverbs 19:20 NKJV

God gives wisdom, knowledge,
and joy to those who please Him.

Ecclesiastes 2:26 NLT

By wisdom a house is built, and by
understanding it is established;
by knowledge the rooms are filled
with all precious and pleasant riches.

Proverbs 24:3-4 ESV

Praise the name of God forever
and ever, for He has all wisdom
and power. He gives wisdom to the
wise and knowledge to the scholars.

Daniel 2:20-21 NLT

The fear of the Lord is the beginning
of wisdom, and knowledge of the
Holy One is understanding.

Proverbs 9:10 NIV

Wisdom will enter your heart,
and knowledge will fill you with joy.
Wise choices will watch over you.
Understanding will keep you safe.
Wisdom will save you from
evil people, from those
whose words are twisted.

Proverbs 2:10-12 NLT

As we
trust God
to give us wisdom
for today's decisions,
He will lead us
a step at a time
into what He
wants us to be
doing in the future.

THEODORE EPP

9.
Words of Wisdom

All Scripture is inspired by God and is useful to teach us what is true and to make us realize what is wrong in our lives. It corrects us when we are wrong and teaches us to do what is right. God uses it to prepare and equip His people to do every good work.

2 Timothy 3:16-17 NLT

Above all, you must understand that no prophecy of Scripture came about by the prophet's own interpretation of things. For prophecy never had its origin in the human will, but prophets, though human, spoke from God as they were carried along by the Holy Spirit.

2 Peter 1:20-21 NIV

Your word, LORD, is eternal; it stands firm in the heavens.

Psalm 119:89 NIV

The entirety of Your word is truth,
and every one of Your righteous
judgments endures forever.

Psalm 119:160 NKJV

"Blessed rather are those who
hear the word of God and obey it."

Luke 11:28 NIV

Jesus answered, "It is written:
'Man shall not live on bread alone,
but on every word that comes from
the mouth of God.'"

Matthew 4:4 NIV

For whatever was written in former
days was written for our instruction,
that through endurance and through
the encouragement of the Scriptures
we might have hope.

Romans 15:4 ESV

"Heaven and earth will pass away,
but My words will never pass away."

Matthew 24:35 NIV

For the word of God is alive
and active. Sharper than any
double-edged sword, it penetrates
even to dividing soul and spirit,
joints and marrow; it judges the
thoughts and attitudes of the heart.

Hebrews 4:12 NIV

"Keep this Book of the Law always
on your lips; meditate on it day and
night, so that you may be careful to
do everything written in it. Then you
will be prosperous and successful."

Joshua 1:8 NIV

Don't just listen to God's word.
You must do what it says.
Otherwise, you are only fooling
yourselves. For if you listen to the
word and don't obey, it is like
glancing at your face in a mirror. You
see yourself, walk away, and forget
what you look like. But if you look
carefully into the perfect law
that sets you free, and if you do
what it says and don't forget what
you heard, then God will
bless you for doing it.

James 1:22-25 NLT

No man is
uneducated who
knows the Bible,
and no one
is wise who
is wise who
is ignorant of its
teachings.

SAMUEL CHADWICK

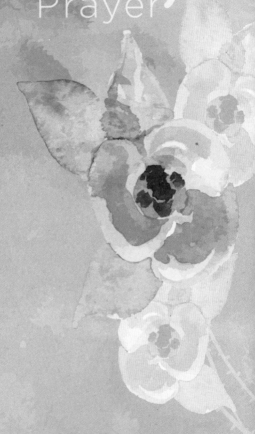

Serenity
Prayer

Living
one day at a time;
enjoying
one moment at a time;

accepting hardships

as the pathway to

peace.

10.
Enjoying Today

This is the day that the Lord has made;
let us rejoice and be glad in it.

Psalm 118:24 ESV

Those who sow with tears
will reap with songs of joy.

Psalm 126:5 NIV

The Lord is my strength and song,
and He has become my salvation.

Psalm 118:14 NKJV

Glory in His holy name; let the hearts
of those who seek the Lord rejoice.

Psalm 105:3 NIV

"Rejoice because your names
are written in heaven."

Luke 10:20 NKJV

"Be happy! Yes, leap for joy!
For a great reward awaits you
in heaven."

Luke 6:23 NLT

In Him our hearts rejoice,
for we trust in His holy name.

Psalm 33:21 NIV

The joy of the Lord is your strength.

Nehemiah 8:10 NKJV

When Your words came, I ate them;
they were my joy and
my heart's delight.

Jeremiah 15:16 NIV

The Lord is my strength and shield.
I trust Him with all my heart.
He helps me, and my heart is filled
with joy. I burst out in songs
of thanksgiving.

Psalm 28:7 NLT

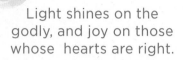

Light shines on the
godly, and joy on those
whose hearts are right.

Psalm 97:11 NLT

You turned my wailing into
dancing; You removed my
sackcloth and clothed me with joy.

Psalm 30:11 NIV

Those who look to Him for help will
be radiant with joy; no shadow of
shame will darken their faces.

Psalm 34:5 NLT

Because You are my help,
I sing in the shadow of Your wings.

Psalm 63:7 NIV

You have given me greater joy than
those who have abundant harvests
of grain and new wine.

Psalm 4:7 NLT

Honor and majesty are before Him;
strength and gladness are
in His place.

1 Chronicles 16:27 NKJV

Keep the joy
of loving God
in your heart
and share
this joy with
all you meet.

MOTHER TERESA

11.
Using My Time Wisely

Be very careful, then, how you live –
not as unwise but as wise, making the
most of every opportunity, because
the days are evil.

Ephesians 5:15-16 NIV

"We must quickly carry out the tasks
assigned us by the One who sent us.
The night is coming, and then
no one can work."

John 9:4 NLT

Teach us to number our days,
that we may gain a heart of wisdom.

Psalm 90:12 NIV

Whether you eat or drink or whatever
you do, do it all for the glory of God.

1 Corinthians 10:31 NIV

Do not boast about tomorrow,
for you do not know what
a day may bring forth.

Proverbs 27:1 NKJV

Be wise in the way you act
toward outsiders; make the most
of every opportunity.

Colossians 4:5 NIV

"We must quickly carry out the
tasks assigned us by the One who
sent us. The night is coming,
and then no one can work."

John 9:4 NLT

We fix our eyes not on what is seen,
but on what is unseen, since what is
seen is temporary, but what is
unseen is eternal.

2 Corinthians 4:18 NIV

My child, listen to me and do as
I say, and you will have a long,
good life.

Proverbs 4:10 NLT

Anyone who belongs
to Christ has become
a new person. The old life
is gone; a new life has begun!

2 Corinthians 5:17 NLT

The LORD keeps you from all
harm and watches over your life.
The LORD keeps watch over you
as you come and go,
both now and forever.

Psalm 121:7-8 NLT

Listen, I tell you a mystery:
We will not all sleep, but we will all
be changed – in a flash, in the
twinkling of an eye, at the last
trumpet. For the trumpet will sound,
the dead will be raised imperishable,
and we will be changed.

1 Corinthians 15:51-52 NIV

Our days may come to seventy
years, or eighty, if our strength
endures; yet the best of them are
but trouble and sorrow, for they
quickly pass, and we fly away.

Psalm 90:10 NIV

Time is lost
when we
have not lived a
full human life,
time unenriched
by experience,
creative endeavor,
enjoyment,
and suffering.

DIETRICH BONHOEFFER

12.
Getting through Hardships

Blessed is the one who perseveres under trial because, having stood the test, that person will receive the crown of life.

James 1:12 NIV

We rejoice in our sufferings, knowing that suffering produces endurance, and endurance produces character, and character produces hope, and hope does not put us to shame, because God's love has been poured into our hearts through the Holy Spirit who has been given to us.

Romans 5:3-5 ESV

The more we suffer for Christ, the more God will shower us with His comfort through Christ.

2 Corinthians 1:5 NLT

God had planned something
better for us.

Hebrews 11:40 NIV

Be strong and do not give up,
for your work will be rewarded.

2 Chronicles 15:7 NIV

The Lord knows how to rescue
godly people from their trials.

2 Peter 2:9 NLT

Since He Himself has gone through
suffering and testing, He is able to
help us when we are being tested.

Hebrews 2:18 NLT

"Don't let your hearts be troubled.
Trust in God, and trust also in Me."

John 14:1 NLT

If you suffer for doing good
and you endure it, this is
commendable before God.

1 Peter 2:20 NIV

The Lord sustains them
on their sickbed and restores
them from their bed of illness.

Psalm 41:3 NIV

I consider that the sufferings
of this present time are not worth
comparing with the glory
that is to be revealed to us.

Romans 8:18 ESV

"In this world you will have trouble.
But take heart!
I have overcome the world."

John 16:33 NIV

"For I am the Lord your God
who takes hold of your right hand
and says to you, 'Do not fear;
I will help you.'"

Isaiah 41:13 NIV

Let us throw off everything that
hinders and the sin that so easily
entangles. And let us run with
perseverance the race marked
out for us.

Hebrews 12:1 NIV

Trials teach us
what we are;
they dig up
the soil,
and let us
see what we
are made of.

CHARLES H. SPURGEON

13.
Overcoming Temptation

Submit to God. Resist the devil
and he will flee from you.

James 4:7 NKJV

Your word I have hidden in my heart,
that I might not sin against You.

Psalm 119:11 NKJV

God blesses those who patiently
endure testing and temptation.
Afterward they will receive the crown
of life that God has promised to those
who love Him. And remember,
when you are being tempted,
do not say, "God is tempting me."
God is never tempted to do wrong,
and He never tempts anyone else.
Temptation comes from our own
desires, which entice us and
drag us away.

James 1:12-14 NLT

This is the love of God,
that we keep His commandments.
And His commandments are not
burdensome. For whatever is born
of God overcomes the world.
And this is the victory that has
overcome the world – our faith.
Who is he who overcomes
the world, but he who believes
that Jesus is the Son of God?

1 John 5:3-5 NKJV

No temptation has overtaken you
that is not common to man.
God is faithful, and He will not let
you be tempted beyond your ability,
but with the temptation He will also
provide the way of escape, that you
may be able to endure it.

1 Corinthians 10:13 ESV

Because He Himself suffered when
He was tempted, He is able to help
those who are being tempted.

Hebrews 2:18 NIV

Be strong in the Lord and in His mighty power. Put on all of God's armor so that you will be able to stand firm against all strategies of the devil. For we are not fighting against flesh-and-blood enemies, but against evil rulers and authorities of the unseen world, against mighty powers in this dark world, and against evil spirits in the heavenly places.

Ephesians 6:10-12 NLT

Since then we have a great High Priest who has passed through the heavens, Jesus, the Son of God, let us hold fast our confession. For we do not have a High Priest who is unable to sympathize with our weaknesses, but one who in every respect has been tempted as we are, yet without sin. Let us then with confidence draw near to the throne of grace, that we may receive mercy and find grace to help in time of need.

Hebrews 4:14-16 ESV

To realize God's presence is the one sovereign remedy against temptation.

FRANÇOIS FÉNELON

14.
The Pathway to Peace

"I am leaving you with a gift –
peace of mind and heart.
And the peace I give is a gift
the world cannot give.
So don't be troubled or afraid."

John 14:27 NLT

"In Me you may have peace.
In the world you will have tribulation;
but be of good cheer,
I have overcome the world."

John 16:33 NKJV

Jesus said, "Come to Me, all of you
who are weary and carry heavy
burdens, and I will give you rest."

Matthew 11:28 NLT

The mind governed by the Spirit
is life and peace.

Romans 8:6 NIV

When people's lives please
the LORD, even their enemies
are at peace with them.

Proverbs 16:7 NLT

The LORD gives strength to
His people; the LORD blesses
His people with peace.

Psalm 29:11 NIV

The peace of God, which surpasses
all understanding, will guard your
hearts and your minds
in Christ Jesus.

Philippians 4:7 NKJV

Great peace have those who love
Your law, and nothing can make
them stumble.

Psalm 119:165 NIV

Let the peace of Christ
rule in your hearts.

Colossians 3:15 ESV

God is not a God of confusion
but of peace.

1 Corinthians 14:33 ESV

You will keep in perfect peace those
whose minds are steadfast,
because they trust in You!

Isaiah 26:3 NIV

The God of peace be with you.

Romans 15:33 NIV

I will both lie down in peace,
and sleep; for You alone, O LORD,
make me dwell in safety.

Psalm 4:8 NKJV

"Glory to God in the highest
heaven, and on earth peace to
those on whom His favor rests."

Luke 2:14 NIV

"Blessed are the peacemakers,
for they shall be called sons of God."

Matthew 5:9 ESV

As we pour out
our bitterness,
God pours in
His peace.

F. B. MEYER

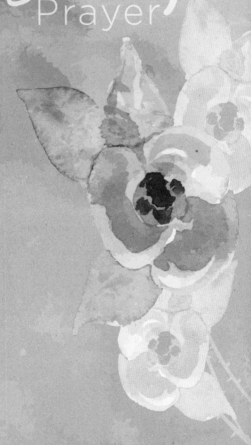

Serenity
Prayer

Taking, as *He* did,

this sinful world as it is,

not as I would have it.

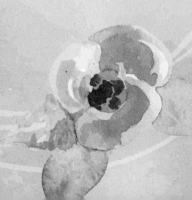

15.
Following Jesus' Example

"If you will obey Me and keep My covenant, you will be My own special treasure from among all the peoples on earth; for all the earth belongs to Me."

Exodus 19:5 NLT

"I am the light of the world. Whoever follows Me will not walk in darkness, but will have the light of life."

John 8:12 ESV

If they obey and serve Him, they shall spend their days in prosperity, and their years in pleasures.

Job 36:11 NKJV

Just as you accepted Christ Jesus as your Lord, you must continue to follow Him.

Colossians 2:6 NLT

"If you love Me, you will keep
My commandments."

John 14:15 ESV

You shall walk after the Lord
your God and fear Him, and keep
His commandments and obey
His voice; you shall serve Him
and hold fast to Him.

Deuteronomy 13:4 NKJV

This is love, that we walk
according to His commandments.
This is the commandment, that as
you have heard from the beginning,
you should walk in it.

2 John 1:6 NKJV

This is what the Lord says – your
Redeemer, the Holy One of Israel:
"I am the Lord your God, who
teaches you what is best for you,
who directs you in the way
you should go."

Isaiah 48:17 NIV

As obedient children, do not conform to the evil desires you had when you lived in ignorance. But just as He who called you is holy, so be holy in all you do; for it is written: "Be holy, because I am holy."

1 Peter 1:14-16 NIV

This is the love of God, that we keep His commandments. And His commandments are not burdensome. For whatever is born of God overcomes the world. And this is the victory that has overcome the world – our faith.

1 John 5:3-5 NKJV

What does the Lord your God require of you, but to fear the Lord your God, to walk in all His ways and to love Him, to serve the Lord your God with all your heart and with all your soul, and to keep the commandments of the Lord and His statutes which I command you today for your good?

Deuteronomy 10:12-13 NKJV

To call yourself
a child of God
is one thing.
To be called
a child of God
by those who
watch your life
is another thing
altogether.

MAX LUCADO

16.
Captive in a Sinful World

Jesus replied, "Very truly I tell you, everyone who sins is a slave to sin. Now a slave has no permanent place in the family, but a son belongs to it forever. So if the Son sets you free, you will be free indeed."

John 8:34-36 NIV

We are all infected and impure with sin. When we display our righteous deeds, they are nothing but filthy rags. Like autumn leaves, we wither and fall, and our sins sweep us away like the wind.

Isaiah 64:6 NLT

The Lord looked down from His sanctuary on high, from heaven He viewed the earth, to hear the groans of the prisoners and release those condemned to death.

Psalm 102:19-20 NIV

For all have sinned and fall short
of the glory of God, and all are
justified freely by His grace
through the redemption that
came by Christ Jesus.

Romans 3:23-24 NIV

Behold, I was brought forth in
iniquity, and in sin my mother
conceived me. Behold, You desire
truth in the inward parts, and in the
hidden part You will make
me to know wisdom.

Psalm 51:5-6 NKJV

When people escape from the
wickedness of the world by knowing
our Lord and Savior Jesus Christ
and then get tangled up and
enslaved by sin again, they are
worse off than before.

2 Peter 2:20 NLT

Surely there is not a righteous man
on earth who does good
and never sins.

Ecclesiastes 7:20 ESV

The Spirit of the Sovereign LORD is upon me, for the LORD has anointed me to bring good news to the poor. He has sent me to comfort the brokenhearted and to proclaim that captives will be released and prisoners will be freed.

Isaiah 61:1 NLT

But thanks be to God, that you who were once slaves of sin have become obedient from the heart to the standard of teaching to which you were committed, and, having been set free from sin, have become slaves of righteousness.

Romans 6:17-18 ESV

If we claim we have not sinned, we are calling God a liar and showing that His word has no place in our hearts.

1 John 1:10 NLT

There is no one who does not sin.

1 Kings 8:46 NIV

The Bible will keep you from sin, or sin will keep you from the Bible.

DWIGHT L. MOODY

17.
Freedom
from Sin

Sin is no longer your master, for you
no longer live under the requirements
of the law. Instead, you live under the
freedom of God's grace.

Romans 6:14 NLT

If the law could give us new life,
we could be made right with God by
obeying it. But the Scriptures declare
that we are all prisoners of sin, so we
receive God's promise of freedom
only by believing in Jesus Christ.

Galatians 3:21-22 NLT

If the Son sets you free,
you will be free indeed.

John 8:36 ESV

Now the Lord is the Spirit,
and where the Spirit of the Lord is,
there is freedom.

2 Corinthians 3:17 ESV

It is for freedom that Christ has set
us free. Stand firm, then, and do not
let yourselves be burdened again
by a yoke of slavery.

Galatians 5:1 NIV

Live as people who are free,
not using your freedom
as a cover-up for evil, but
living as servants of God.

1 Peter 2:16 ESV

He will keep you strong to the end
so that you will be free from all
blame on the day when our
Lord Jesus Christ returns. God will
do this, for He is faithful to do what
He says, and He has invited you into
partnership with His Son,
Jesus Christ our Lord.

1 Corinthians 1:8-9 NLT

To Him who loves us and has freed
us from our sins by His blood,
to Him be glory and power
for ever and ever!

Revelation 1:5-6 NIV

You are free from your slavery
to sin, and you have become
slaves to righteous living.

Romans 6:18 NLT

He gave His life to free us
from every kind of sin,
to cleanse us, and to make us
His very own people, totally
committed to doing good deeds.

Titus 2:14 NLT

Lord, I am Your servant; yes, I am
Your servant, born into Your
household; You have freed me from
my chains. I will offer You a
sacrifice of thanksgiving and
call on the name of the Lord.

Psalm 116:16-17 NLT

For the law of the Spirit of life
in Christ Jesus has made me free
from the law of sin and death.

Romans 8:2 NKJV

Christian liberty
is freedom
from sin,
not freedom
to sin.

A. W. TOZER

18.
The Importance of Forgiveness

"I have blotted out, like a thick cloud, your transgressions, and like a cloud, your sins. Return to Me, for I have redeemed you."

Isaiah 44:22 NKJV

As far as the east is from the west, so far has He removed our transgressions from us.

Psalm 103:12 NIV

"I will forgive their wickedness, and I will never again remember their sins."

Hebrews 8:12 NLT

"Though your sins are like scarlet, they shall be as white as snow; though they are red as crimson, they shall be like wool."

Isaiah 1:18 NIV

The Lord our God is merciful
and forgiving.

Daniel 9:9 NLT

All the prophets testify about Him
that everyone who believes in Him
receives forgiveness of sins
through His name.

Acts 10:43 NIV

It is the power of God that brings
salvation to everyone who believes.

Romans 1:16 NIV

If anyone sins, we have an
Advocate with the Father,
Jesus Christ the righteous.
And He Himself is the propitiation
for our sins, and not for ours only
but also for the whole world.

1 John 2:1-2 NKJV

"Be encouraged, My child!
Your sins are forgiven."

Matthew 9:2 NLT

You are a forgiving God,
gracious and compassionate,
slow to anger and
abounding in love.

Nehemiah 9:17 NIV

He has delivered us from the domain
of darkness and transferred us to
the kingdom of His beloved Son,
in whom we have redemption,
the forgiveness of sins.

Colossians 1:13-14 ESV

The LORD is my light and my
salvation – whom shall I fear?
The LORD is the stronghold of my
life – of whom shall I be afraid?

Psalm 27:1 NIV

Now there is no condemnation for
those who belong to Christ Jesus.
And because you belong to Him,
the power of the life-giving Spirit
has freed you from the power of sin
that leads to death.

Romans 8:1-2 NLT

When
God forgives,
He at once
restores.

THEODORE EPP

19.
Victory over Sin

Thanks be to God! He gives us the victory through our Lord Jesus Christ.

1 Corinthians 15:57 NIV

Some nations boast of their chariots and horses, but we boast in the name of the Lᴏʀᴅ our God. Those nations will fall down and collapse, but we will rise up and stand firm.

Psalm 20:7-8 NLT

The Lᴏʀᴅ shall go forth like a mighty man; He shall stir up His zeal like a man of war. He shall cry out, yes, shout aloud; He shall prevail against His enemies.

Isaiah 42:13 NKJV

Victory comes from You, O Lᴏʀᴅ. May You bless Your people.

Psalm 3:8 NLT

Thanks be to God who always
leads us in triumph in Christ,
and through us diffuses
the fragrance of His knowledge
in every place.

2 Corinthians 2:14 NKJV

Songs of joy and victory are sung
in the camp of the godly.
The strong right arm of the Lord
has done glorious things!

Psalm 118:15 NLT

The Lord your God is the one
who goes with you to fight for you
against your enemies
to give you victory.

Deuteronomy 20:4 NIV

We know that God causes
everything to work together
for the good of those who love
God and are called according
to His purpose for them.

Romans 8:28 NLT

He has delivered me from
every trouble, and my eye has
looked in triumph on my enemies.

Psalm 54:7 ESV

The horse is made ready
for the day of battle, but the
victory belongs to the LORD.

Proverbs 21:31 ESV

Through God we will do valiantly,
for it is He who shall tread down
our enemies.

Psalm 60:12 NKJV

The LORD gives victory to His
anointed. He answers him from
His heavenly sanctuary with the
victorious power of His right hand.

Psalm 20:6 NIV

I put no trust in my bow, my sword
does not bring me victory; but You
give us victory over our enemies,
You put our adversaries to shame.

Psalm 44:6-7 NIV

Long-lasting victory can never be separated from a long-lasting stand on the foundation of the cross.

WATCHMAN NEE

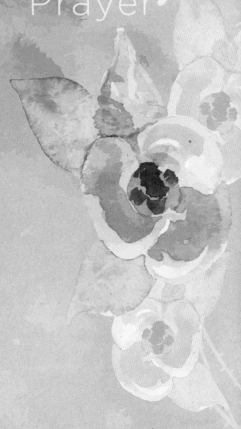

Serenity
Prayer

Trusting
that He will
make all things *right*
if I surrender to His
Will.

20.
Trusting God

The LORD is good, a refuge in times
of trouble. He cares for those
who trust in Him.

Nahum 1:7 NIV

Trust in the LORD forever, for the
LORD GOD is an everlasting rock.

Isaiah 26:4 ESV

May the God of hope fill you with all
joy and peace as you trust in Him,
so that you may overflow with hope
by the power of the Holy Spirit.

Romans 15:13 NIV

It is better to take refuge in the
LORD than to trust in people.

Psalm 118:8 NLT

Blessed is the one
who trusts in the LORD.

Psalm 40:4 NIV

Trust in Him at all times, you people;
pour out your heart before Him;
God is a refuge for us.

Psalm 62:8 NKJV

Blessed is the one who trusts in the
LORD, whose confidence is in Him.

Jeremiah 17:7 NIV

Put your trust in the LORD.

Psalm 4:5 ESV

Some trust in chariots and some
in horses, but we trust in
the name of the LORD our God.

Psalm 20:7 NIV

If we are faithful to the end, trusting
God just as firmly as when we first
believed, we will share in all that
belongs to Christ.

Hebrews 3:14 NLT

The LORD is righteous in all His ways
and faithful in all He does.

Psalm 145:17 NIV

As Scripture says,
"Anyone who believes in Him
will never be put to shame."

Romans 10:11 NIV

"I will rescue those who love Me.
I will protect those who trust
in My name."

Psalm 91:14 NLT

Trust in the Lord, and do good;
dwell in the land, and feed on
His faithfulness.

Psalm 37:3 NKJV

Those who know Your name trust in
You, for You, Lord, have never
forsaken those who seek You.

Psalm 9:10 NIV

The fear of man brings a snare,
but whoever trusts in the Lord
shall be safe.

Proverbs 29:25 NKJV

Those who listen to instruction
will prosper; those who trust
the Lord will be joyful.

Proverbs 16:20 NLT

*Trust the past
to God's mercy,
the present to God's
love and the future
to God's providence.*

ST. AUGUSTINE

21.
God Will Make Things Right

The LORD is good to everyone.
He showers compassion on all
His creation. All of Your works will
thank You, LORD, and Your faithful
followers will praise You.

Psalm 145:9-10 NLT

Just then a man came up to Jesus
and asked, "Teacher, what good thing
must I do to get eternal life?"
"Why do you ask Me about what is
good?" Jesus replied. "There is only
One who is good. If you want to enter
life, keep the commandments."

Matthew 19:16-17 NIV

His divine power has given us
everything we need for a godly life
through our knowledge of Him
who called us by His own glory
and goodness.

2 Peter 1:3 NIV

"Why do you call Me good?"
Jesus asked. "Only God
is truly good."

Mark 10:18 NLT

You are good, and what You do is
good; teach me Your decrees.

Psalm 119:68 NIV

Truly God is good to Israel,
to such as are pure in heart.

Psalm 73:1 NKJV

For You, O Lord, are good and
forgiving, abounding in steadfast
love to all who call upon You.

Psalm 86:5 ESV

Praise the LORD, for the LORD is good;
sing to His name, for it is pleasant!

Psalm 135:3 ESV

The earth is full of the
goodness of the LORD.

Psalm 33:5 NKJV

Good and upright is the Lᴏʀᴅ;
therefore He instructs sinners
in His ways. He guides the humble
in what is right and teaches
them His way.

Psalm 25:8-9 NIV

Every good gift and every perfect gift
is from above, and comes down from
the Father of lights, with whom there
is no variation or shadow of turning.

James 1:17 NKJV

The Lᴏʀᴅ will do what is good
in His sight.

2 Samuel 10:12 NIV

The Lᴏʀᴅ is good, a strong refuge
when trouble comes. He is close to
those who trust in Him.

Nahum 1:7 NLT

Give thanks to the Lᴏʀᴅ, for He is
good; His love endures forever.

Psalm 106:1 NIV

The goodness
of God is
infinitely more
wonderful than
we will ever
be able to
comprehend.

A. W. TOZER

22.
God's Perfect Will

Be thankful in all circumstances,
for this is God's will for you who
belong to Christ Jesus.

1 Thessalonians 5:18 NLT

Do not be conformed to this world,
but be transformed by the renewal of
your mind, that by testing you may
discern what is the will of God, what is
good and acceptable and perfect.

Romans 12:2 ESV

"This is the only work God wants from
you: Believe in the One He has sent."

John 6:29 NLT

For this is the will of God, that by
doing good you should put to silence
the ignorance of foolish people.

1 Peter 2:15 ESV

Be filled with the Holy Spirit,
singing psalms and hymns and
spiritual songs among yourselves,
and making music to the Lord in
your hearts. And give thanks for
everything to God the Father in the
name of our Lord Jesus Christ.

Ephesians 5:18-20 NLT

Do not be foolish, but understand
what the will of the Lord is.

Ephesians 5:17 ESV

You can make many plans, but the
Lord's purpose will prevail.

Proverbs 19:21 NLT

"Whoever does the will of God, he is
My brother and sister and mother."

Mark 3:35 ESV

God's will is for you to be holy, so
stay away from all sexual sin. Then
each of you will control his own
body and live in holiness and honor.

1 Thessalonians 4:3-4 NLT

You need to persevere so that when
you have done the will of God,
you will receive what
He has promised.

Hebrews 10:35-36 NKJV

The Father who knows all hearts
knows what the Spirit is saying, for
the Spirit pleads for us believers in
harmony with God's own will.

Romans 8:27 NLT

"For I have come down from
heaven to do the will of God who
sent Me, not to do My own will.
And this is the will of God,
that I should not lose even one of
all those He has given Me, but that
I should raise them up at the last
day. For it is My Father's will that
all who see His Son and believe in
Him should have eternal life."

John 6:38-40 NLT

There are no "ifs" in God's world. And no places that are safer than other places. The center of His will is our only safety – let us pray that we may always know it!

CORRIE TEN BOOM

23.
Obeying His Will

Peter and the other apostles replied:
"We must obey God rather than
human beings!

Acts 5:29 NIV

Obey the LORD your God and follow
His commands and decrees.

Deuteronomy 27:10 NIV

For merely listening to the law
doesn't make us right with God.
It is obeying the law that makes
us right in His sight.

Romans 2:13 NLT

Thanks be to God that, though you
used to be slaves to sin, you have
come to obey from your heart
the pattern of teaching that has
now claimed your allegiance.

Romans 6:17 NIV

"Obey My voice, and I will be your
God, and you shall be My people.
And walk in all the ways that I have
commanded you, that it may
be well with you."

Jeremiah 7:23 NKJV

You must love the LORD your God
and always obey His requirements,
decrees, regulations, and commands.

Deuteronomy 11:1 NLT

Jesus replied, "All who love Me will
do what I say. My Father will love
them, and we will come and make
our home with each of them."

John 14:23 NLT

If you fully obey the LORD your God
and carefully follow all His
commands I give you today,
the LORD your God will set you high
above all the nations on earth.

Deuteronomy 28:1 NIV

Do not merely listen
to the word, and so deceive
yourselves. Do what it says.

James 1:22 NIV

You shall walk in all the ways which
the Lord your God has commanded
you, that you may live and that it may
be well with you, and that you may
prolong your days in the land
which you shall possess.

Deuteronomy 5:33 NKJV

Study this Book of Instruction
continually. Meditate on it day and
night so you will be sure to obey
everything written in it. Only then will
you prosper and succeed in all you do.

Joshua 1:8 NLT

Observe the requirements of the
Lord your God, and follow all
His ways. Keep the decrees,
commands, regulations, and laws written in the Law of Moses so that you
will be successful in all you do
and wherever you go.

1 Kings 2:3 NLT

Being a Christian
is less about
cautiously avoiding
sin than about
courageously
and actively
doing God's will.

DIETRICH BONHOEFFER

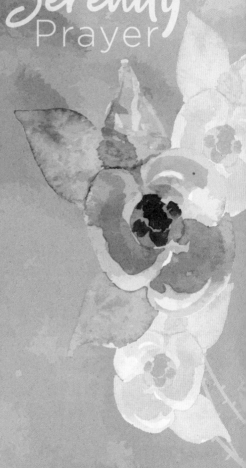

Serenity
Prayer

That I may be
reasonably *happy*
in this life and supremely

happy with *Him*

forever in the next.
Amen.

24.

Being Content in this Life

The righteous eat to their hearts'
content, but the stomach of
the wicked goes hungry.

Proverbs 13:25 NIV

True godliness with contentment
is itself great wealth.

1 Timothy 6:6 NLT

For we brought nothing into this
world, and it is certain we can
carry nothing out. And having food
and clothing, with these
we shall be content.

1 Timothy 6:7-8 NKJV

Those who love money will never
have enough. How meaningless to
think that wealth brings
true happiness!

Ecclesiastes 5:10 NLT

The fear of the Lord leads to life;
then one rests content,
untouched by trouble.

Proverbs 19:23 NIV

Enjoy what you have rather than
desiring what you don't have.
Just dreaming about nice things is
meaningless – like chasing the wind.

Ecclesiastes 6:9 NLT

"Beware! Guard against every kind
of greed. Life is not measured by
how much you own."

Luke 12:15 NLT

Better the little that the righteous
have than the wealth
of many wicked.

Psalm 37:16 NIV

Keep your lives free from the love
of money and be content with what
you have, because God has said,
"Never will I leave you;
never will I forsake you."

Hebrews 13:5 NIV

A sound heart is life to the body,
but envy is rottenness to the bones.

Proverbs 14:30 NKJV

A greedy man stirs up strife,
but the one who trusts
in the Lord will be enriched.

Proverbs 28:25 ESV

Better to have little, with godliness,
than to be rich and dishonest.

Proverbs 16:8 NLT

The backslider in heart will be
filled with the fruit of his ways,
and a good man will be filled
with the fruit of his ways.

Proverbs 14:14 ESV

The Lord is my shepherd;
I shall not want. He makes
me lie down in green pastures.
He leads me beside still waters.

Psalm 23:1-2 ESV

It is not
how much
we have,
but how much
we enjoy,
that makes
happiness.

CHARLES H. SPURGEON

25.
Focusing on the Things Above

Let the hearts of those who seek the LORD rejoice! Seek the LORD and His strength; seek His presence continually! Remember the wondrous works that He has done, His miracles and the judgments He uttered.
He is the LORD our God;
His judgments are in all the earth.

1 Chronicles 16:10-12, 14 ESV

I seek You with all my heart; do not let me stray from Your commands.

Psalm 119:10 NIV

Let all those who seek You rejoice and be glad in You; let such as love Your salvation say continually, "The LORD be magnified!"

Psalm 40:16 NKJV

The Lord looks down from heaven
on all mankind to see if there are any
who understand, any who seek God.

Psalm 14:2 NIV

Those who know Your name will put
their trust in You; for You,
Lord, have not forsaken those
who seek You.

Psalm 9:10 NKJV

My heart says of You, "Seek His
face!" Your face, Lord, I will seek.
Do not hide Your face from me,
do not turn Your servant away in
anger; You have been my helper.

Psalm 27:8-9 NIV

Seek the Lord your God, and you
will find Him if you seek Him with all
your heart and with all your soul.

Deuteronomy 4:29 NKJV

Draw near to God,
and He will draw near to you.

James 4:8 ESV

"Ask, and it will be given to you; seek, and you will find; knock, and it will be opened to you. For everyone who asks receives, and the one who seeks finds, and to the one who knocks it will be opened."

Matthew 7:7-8 ESV

"Whoever believes in Me, as Scripture has said, rivers of living water will flow from within them." By this He meant the Spirit, whom those who believed in Him were later to receive.

John 7:38-39 NIV

The LORD is with you while you are with Him. If you seek Him, He will be found by you, but if you forsake Him, He will forsake you.

2 Chronicles 15:2 ESV

The lions may grow weak and hungry, but those who seek the LORD lack no good thing.

Psalm 34:10 NIV

Aim at heaven
and you will get
earth thrown in.
Aim at earth
and you get neither.

C. S. LEWIS

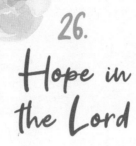

26.
Hope in the Lord

Those who hope in the Lord will renew
their strength. They will soar on wings
like eagles; they will run and not grow
weary, they will walk and not be faint.

Isaiah 40:31 NIV

Blessed are those whose hope
is in the Lord their God.

Psalm 146:5 NIV

May the God of hope fill you with all
joy and peace as you trust in Him,
so that you may overflow with hope
by the power of the Holy Spirit.

Romans 15:13 NIV

Having hope will give you courage.
You will be protected
and will rest in safety.

Job 11:18 NLT

We have this hope as an anchor for the soul, firm and secure. It enters the inner sanctuary behind the curtain, where our forerunner, Jesus, has entered on our behalf.

Hebrews 6:19-20 NIV

Hope will not lead to disappointment. For we know how dearly God loves us, because He has given us the Holy Spirit to fill our hearts with His love.

Romans 5:5 NLT

Hope in the Lord! For with the Lord there is steadfast love, and with Him is plentiful redemption.

Psalm 130:7 ESV

The eye of the Lord is on those who fear Him, on those who hope in His steadfast love.

Psalm 33:18 ESV

My help comes from the Lord, who made heaven and earth!

Psalm 121:2 NLT

You answer us with awesome
deeds of righteousness,
O God our Savior, the hope
of all the ends of the earth and
of the farthest seas.

Psalm 65:5 NIV

I pray that the eyes of your heart
may be enlightened in order that
you may know the hope to which
He has called you.

Ephesians 1:18 NIV

I saw the Lord always before me ...
therefore my heart is glad and my
tongue rejoices; my body also will
live in hope.

Acts 2:25-26 NIV

The needy shall not always be
forgotten, and the hope of the
poor shall not perish forever.

Psalm 9:18 ESV

Hope deferred makes the heart sick,
but a dream fulfilled is a tree of life.

Proverbs 13:12 NLT

Hope
is one of the
principal springs
that keep mankind
in motion.

THOMAS FULLER

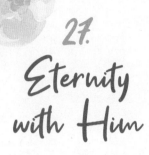

27.
Eternity
with Him

"Truly, truly, I say to you,
whoever believes has eternal life."

John 6:47 ESV

Whoever has the Son has life;
whoever does not have the
Son of God does not have life.

1 John 5:12 ESV

"My Father's will is that everyone who
looks to the Son and believes in Him
shall have eternal life."

John 6:40 NIV

"God so loved the world that He gave
His only begotten Son, that whoever
believes in Him should not perish
but have everlasting life."

John 3:16 NKJV

"Everyone who lives in Me and believes in Me will never ever die."

John 11:26 NLT

For the wages of sin is death, but the free gift of God is eternal life through Christ Jesus our Lord.

Romans 6:23 NLT

"Indeed, the time is coming when all the dead in their graves will hear the voice of God's Son, and they will rise again. Those who have done good will rise to experience eternal life, and those who have continued in evil will rise to experience judgment."

John 5:28-29 NLT

"I give them eternal life, and they shall never perish; no one will snatch them out of My hand. My Father, who has given them to Me, is greater than all; no one can snatch them out of My Father's hand. I and the Father are one."

John 10:28-30 NIV

"You can enter God's Kingdom
only through the narrow gate.
The highway to hell is broad,
and its gate is wide for the many
who choose that way. But the
gateway to life is very narrow
and the road is difficult,
and only a few ever find it."

Matthew 7:13-14 NLT

Therefore we do not lose heart.
Even though our outward man is
perishing, yet the inward man is
being renewed day by day.
For our light affliction, which is
but for a moment, is working for us
a far more exceeding and
eternal weight of glory.

2 Corinthians 4:16-17 NKJV

He who believes in the Son has
everlasting life; and he who does
not believe the Son shall not see life,
but the wrath of God abides on him.

John 3:36 NKJV

Eternal life
does not start when
we go to heaven.
It starts the moment
you reach out
to Jesus.
He never turns
His back on anyone.
And He is waiting
for you.

CORRIE TEN BOOM

28.
A Place in Heaven

"In My Father's house are many mansions; if it were not so, I would have told you. I go to prepare a place for you. And if I go and prepare a place for you, I will come again and receive you to Myself; that where I am, there you may be also."

John 14:2-3 NKJV

For we know that if the tent that is our earthly home is destroyed, we have a building from God, a house not made with hands, eternal in the heavens.

2 Corinthians 5:1 ESV

"No eye has seen, no ear has heard, and no mind has imagined what God has prepared for those who love Him."

1 Corinthians 2:9 NLT

"Then the King will say to those on His right hand, 'Come, you blessed of My Father, inherit the kingdom prepared for you from the foundation of the world: for I was hungry and you gave Me food;
I was thirsty and you gave Me drink;
I was a stranger.and you took Me in;
I was naked and you clothed Me;
I was sick and you visited Me;
I was in prison and you came to Me.'"

Matthew 25:34-36 NKJV

Jesus answered him,
"Truly I tell you, today you will be with Me in paradise."

Luke 23:43 NIV

"People will come from all over the world – from east and west, north and south – to take their places in the Kingdom of God. And note this: Some who seem least important now will be the greatest then, and some who are the greatest now will be least important then."

Luke 13:29-30 NLT

God destines
us for an end
beyond the grasp
of reason.

THOMAS AQUINAS